2
Hadith

Selections from

Bukhari, Muslim, Tirmidhi
Abu Dawood, Ibn Maja,
Al-Bayhaqi

Islamic Book Service (P) Ltd.
New Delhi

200 HADITH

ISBN 978-81-7231-308-1

First Published 2001
Seventh Impression 2021

Published by *Abdus Sami* for

Islamic Book Service (P) Ltd.

1516-18, Pataudi House, Darya Ganj, New Delhi-2 (India)
Tel.: +91-11-23244556, 23253514, 23286551
e-mail: info@ibsbookstore.com
Website: www.ibsbookstore.com

Our Associates
Husami Book Depot, Hyderabad (India)

Printed in India

"SO TAKE WHAT THE
APOSTLE
ASSIGNS TO YOU, AND DENY
YOURSELVES THAT WHICH HE
WITHHOLDS FROM YOU".

AL-QUR'AN - ALHASHR: 7

FOREWORD

The present volume is an anthology compiled from the Ḥadīth literature, an Islamic source second only to the Qur'ān in religious importance. Although brief, it covers, directly, the more important aspects of the Ḥadīth's teachings. The sayings of the Prophet Muḥammad ﷺ have been handed down to posterity through both oral and written traditions, the foundations of which were laid by the Prophet's Companions, some of whom were also his scribes.

The followings are some of the principles by which he sought to guide his followers. Eternal in essence, they are of value not only to Muslims, but to humanity at large.

1

Islam has been built on five pillars:
testifying that there is no god but Allah and
Muuḥammad is His Messenger;
performance of prayers; alms-giving (zakāt);
pilgrimage to the Kaʻbah;
fasting during Ramaḍān.

ḤADĪTH OF AL-BUKHĀRĪ AND MUSLIM
ON THE AUTHORITY OF ʻABDULLĀH IBN ʻUMAR.

2

Anyone who befriends another
or makes an enemy, gives or withholds, has
perfected his faith, if what he does is done
for the sake of the Almighty.

ḤADĪTH OF AL-BUKHĀRĪ
ON THE AUTHORITY OF ABŪ UMĀMAH.

3

When the Prophet Muḥammad ﷺ was
asked by ʿAmr ibn ʿAbasah what was meant
by faith, he replied,
'Self-restraint and gentleness.'

ḤADĪTH OF MUSLIM.

4

One who is willing to accept God as his
Lord; Islam as his religion
and Muḥammad as God's Messenger has
savoured the taste of faith.

ḤADĪTH OF AL-BUKHĀRĪ AND MUSLIM ON THE
AUTHORITY OF AL-ʿABBĀS IBN
ʿABD AL-MUṬṬALIB.

5

Simplicity, too, is a part of faith.

ḤADĪTH OF ABŪ DĀWŪD
ON THE AUTHORITY OF ABŪ UMĀMAH.

6

A man without trust is a man without faith.
And a man who does not fulfill his promises
is a man without faith.

HADĪTH OF AHMAD IBN HANBAL.
ON THE AUTHORITY OF ANAS IBN MĀLIK,

7

Greed and faith can never co-exist in the
human heart.

HADĪTH OF AN-NASA'Ī
ON THE AUTHORITY OF ABŪ HURAYRAH.

8

God loves those believers who labour to earn
a living through lawful means.

HADĪTH OF AT-TABARĀNĪ ON THE AUTHORITY OF
'ABDULLĀH IBN 'UMAR.

9

Actions are judged by their intention and every man shall be judged accordingly. Thus he whose migration was for Allah and His Messenger; his migration was for Allah and His Messenger; and he whose migration was to achieve some worldly benefit or to take some women in marriage, his migration was for that for which he migrated.

HADĪTH OF AL-BUKHĀRĪ AND MUSLIM
ON THE AUTHORITY OF ʿUMAR IBN AL-KHAṬṬĀB.

10

When you see sycophants, throw dust in their faces.

HADĪTH OF MUSLIM
ON THE AUTHORITY OF MIQDĀD IBN ASWAD.

11

Asked what reward there would be for a
man who desired fame and compensation
for having performed *jihad*,
the Prophet said, 'there is no reward for him.'
When asked the same question three times
over, the Prophet gave the same reply each
time. Then he said, 'God accepts those deeds
which were performed purely for His sake
and which were meant to seek His pleasure.'

ḤADĪTH OF ABŪ DĀWŪD AND AN-NASĀ'Ī ON THE
AUTHORITY OF ABŪ UMĀMAH.

12

Keep your faith pure. Even the smallest good
deed will suffice.

ACCORDING TO AL-MUNDHIRĪ WHEN
MU'ADH IBN JABAL WAS APPOINTED RULER OF
YEMEN, HE ASKED THE PROPHET FOR ADVICE
AND WAS GIVEN THE ABOVE REPLY.

13

One who says his prayers (*ṣalāt*) with
great propriety when he is in the
presence of others,
but does so without proper reverence
when he is alone, is committing
an act of contempt for his Lord.

ḤADĪTH OF AL-MUNDHIRĪ
ON THE AUTHORITY OF ʿABDULLĀH IBN MASʿŪD.

14

When a person repents,
God's pleasure at this is even greater
than that of one who dismounts
from his camel, loses it in the desert
and then finds it again all of a sudden.

ḤADĪTH OF AL-BUKHĀRĪ AND MUSLIM
ON THE AUTHORITY OF ANAS IBN MĀLIK.

According to 'Amr ibn al-'Āṣ,
the Prophet Muḥammad sent word to him
to come clad in armour
and bearing arms.
When I came into his presence,
he was performing his ablutions.'
The Prophet said to me, 'O 'Amr,
I am sending you on a mission.
God will bring you back safe and will
reward you with spoils.' I said,
'O Prophet, I did not migrate for the spoils.
It was for the sake of God and
His Messenger.' The Prophet replied,
'The best wealth for a good man to
possess is that which has been lawfully
acquired.'

ḤADĪTH OF AḤMAD IBN ḤANBAL.

16

None of you truly believes until your own
inclinations are in accordance with the
message I have brought.

ḤADĪTH QUOTED BY AN-NAWAWĪ FROM *KITĀB AL-
HUJJAH* ON THE AUTHORITY OF ʿABDULLĀH IBN
ʿAMR IBN AL-ʿAṢ

17

God has imposed certain
moral obligations, do not abrogate them;
He has forbidden certain things, do not
indulge in them; He has laid down certain
limits, do not transgress them;
He is silent on certain matters, do not
knowingly argue over them.

ḤADĪTH OF AD-DARQUTNĪ
ON THE AUTHORITY OF ABŪ THAʿLABAH.

18

There is a covenant of *ṣalāt* (prayers)
between me and the people. Therefore,
if a man gives up *ṣalāt*,
he is guilty of *kufr* (infidelity).

ḤADĪTH OF AḤMAD, AT-TIRMIDHĪ, AN-NASĀʾĪ
AND IBN MĀJAH ON THE AUTHORITY OF
BURAYDAH.

19

'Umar ibn al-Khaṭṭāb wrote to
his governors that the most important thing
of all to him was prayer (*ṣalāt*).
A man who prayed regularly safeguarded his
faith. And a man who was found wanting in
his prayers would be found wanting even
more in other matters.

MISHKĀT AL-MAṢĀBĪḤ.

20

A ṣalāt offered in congregation
is 27 times more worthy of
reward than the ṣalāt offered alone.

ḤADĪTH OF AL-BUKHĀRĪ AND MUSLIM
ON THE AUTHORITY OF 'ABDULLĀH IBN 'UMAR.

21

Anywhere that three Muslims reside,
the prayer must be offered
in congregation, otherwise Satan will over-
power them.
Adhere, therefore, to congregational prayer,
lest the wolf eat up the goat which strays
away from the herd.

ḤADĪTH BY ABŪ DĀWŪD
ON THE AUTHORITY OF ABŪ'D-DARDĀ.

22

When you lead the prayer,
you should make it short because,
among those offering *salāt* there may be
some who are infirm, sick and old.
But when you offer individual prayers,
you may lengthen them
as much as you wish.

ḤADĪTH OF AL-BUKHĀRĪ
ON THE AUTHORITY OF ABŪ HURAYRAH.

23

When I stand for *salāt*, I want to
offer a long prayer, but I shorten it when I
hear a child's cry, because I do not want to
cause anxiety to the mother.

ḤADĪTH OF AL-BUKHĀRĪ
ON THE AUTHORITY OF ABŪ QATĀDAH.

24

Jābir ibn Samurah related how he used
to offer Friday prayers with the Prophet.
He said that the latter's prayer,
as well as his sermon were
moderate in length.

ḤADĪTH OF MUSLIM.

25

Everything has a cleansing agent.
And fasting is the cleansing agent
for the body. Fasting is
more a matter of patience
than of anything else.

ḤADĪTH OF IBN MĀJAH
ON THE AUTHORITY OF ABŪ HURAYRAH.

26

If the observer of a fast does not give up
false utterances and their pursuit,
then God does not require him
to give up his food and water.

ḤADĪTH OF AL-BUKHĀRĪ AND MUSLIM
ON THE AUTHORITY OF ABŪ HURAYRAH.

27

Fasting is like a shield.
When one of you is observing a fast,
neither should you indulge in indecent talk
nor should you create an uproar. And if
someone talks ill of you, or fights with you,
you should just say, 'I am observing my fast.'

ḤADĪTH OF AL-BUKHĀRĪ AND MUSLIM
ON THE AUTHORITY OF ABŪ HURAYRAH.

28

The man who keeps a fast in full faith,
and for reward in the world hereafter,
will be forgiven his past sins. And the man
who prays in the night during Ramaḍān with
faith and for reward in the world hereafter,
will be forgiven all his past sins.

HADĪTH OF AL-BUKHĀRĪ AND MUSLIM
ON THE AUTHORITY OF ABŪ HURAYRAH.

29

When Ramaḍān comes, the doors of Heaven
are opened, the doors of Hell are closed, the
devils are put in chains, and the doors of
mercy are opened.

HADĪTH OF AL-BUKHĀRĪ. AND MUSLIM
ON THE AUTHORITY OF ABŪ HURAYRAH.

30

Anas ibn Mālik said that they used to
travel with the Prophet.
Those who observed a fast never
found fault with those who did not keep
the fast. Similarly, those not observing
the fast never said anything
amiss to those who kept their fast.

ḤADĪTH OF AL-BUKHĀRĪ

31

Any man who misses a fast without
a reason, such as illness, can never
atone for it, even if he fasts
for the rest of his life.

ḤADĪTH OF AT-TIRMIDHĪ AND ABŪ DĀWŪD
ON THE AUTHORITY OF ABŪ HURAYRAH.

32

Partake of *saḥūr* (food, taken a little
before dawn during Ramaḍān),
for there is a blessing in it.

ḤADĪTH OF AL-BUKHĀRĪ AND MUSLIM
ON THE AUTHORITY OF ANAS IBN MĀLIK.

33

'Abdullāh ibn al-'Abbās reported
that the Prophet made alms-giving
on 'Īd-ul-Fiṭr an obligatory act.
As well as providing food for the poor,
it was meant to atone for any absurdity
or immodesty that may have been
committed during fasting in the month of
Ramaḍān.

ḤADĪTH OF ABŪ DĀWŪD

34

When you pay *zakāt* (alms),
you have done your duty,
as is obligatory.
But a person who amasses
unlawful wealth and
then makes gifts to the poor
from it will have no spiritual reward
for so doing.
On the contrary,
he will carry the burden
of it with him into the
next world.

ḤADĪTH OF IBN MĀJAH
ON THE AUTHORITY OF ABŪ HURAYRAH.

35

Allah has made the Muslims
duty bound to pay *zakāt* (alms).
It will be released from the wealthy to be
distributed among the needy.

ḤADĪTH OF AL-BUKHĀRĪ AND MUSLIM ON THE
AUTHORITY OF ʿABDULLĀH IBN AL-ʿABBĀS.

36

The owner of any land which is irrigated
by rain water or a stream,
or which is situated close to a river,
is obliged to give one tenth of its
produce to the needy. The owner of
such land as is irrigated by other methods
will pay half this amount.

ḤADĪTH OF AL-BUKHĀRĪ ON THE AUTHORITY
OF ʿABDULLĀH IBN AL-ʿABBĀS.

If a person to whom God
has given wealth
does not give *zakāt* (alms),
he will find that,
on the Day of judgment,
his wealth turns into a poisonous snake
with two black spots on its head.
It will be like a yoke around his neck.
Then it will seize him by the jaws
and declare,
'I am your wealth.
I am your treasure.'

ḤADĪTH OF AL-BUKHĀRĪ
ON THE AUTHORITY OF ABŪ HURAYRAH.

38

A believer, who feeds another
of the faithful who is hungry,
will be fed on the fruits of
Paradise by God on the
Day of judgment.
And a believer,
who serves water to another who is thirsty,
will have his thirst slaked from the sealed
drinks by God on the Day of judgment.
And if a believer clothes another
of the faithful who is in
dire need of clothing,
he too will be rewarded with apparel
from Paradise by God on the
Day of judgment.

ḤADĪTH OF AT-TIRMIDHĪ
ON THE AUTHORITY OF ABŪ SAʿĪD AL-KHUDRĪ.

39

Abū Dharr al-Ghifārī relates that
he came to the Prophet,
who was sitting
in the shade of the Ka'bah.
When he saw me he said,
'They stand to lose.' I said,
'May my parents ransom you.
To whom do you refer?'
'To those with an excess of riches,'
he replied, 'who just squander
their wealth, heedless of the fact that
they can be saved only if they spend
generously for a good cause.
And there are very few
wealthy men of that ilk.'

ḤADĪTH OF AL-BUKHĀRĪ AND MUSLIM.

40

Giving alms to the poor
is a single good deed,
but giving alms to a poor relative has the
double virtue of giving alms and,
at the same time,
treating one's own relative well.

ḤADĪTH OF AN-NASĀ·Ī AND AT-TIRMIDHĪ
ON THE AUTHORITY OF SALMĀN IBN ·ĀMIR.

41

If a man who sets out with the
intention of performing Ḥajj, *umrah* or *jihād*
meets with his death on the way, he will be
granted the rewards of *jihād*, Ḥajj
or *umrah* by his Maker.

ḤADĪTH OF AL-BAYHAQĪ
ON THE AUTHORITY OF ABŪ HURAYRAH.

42

Asked which deed inspired the greatest
respect, the Prophet replied,
'To believe in Allah and
His Messenger.'
When asked what ranked next in order
of merit, he said,
'To perform *jihād*
for the sake of Allah.'
Asked what came after that,
he replied *ḥajj mabrūr*,
that is,
performing pilgrimage
while remaining free from sin.

ḤADĪTH OF AL-BUKHĀRĪ AND MUSLIM
ON THE AUTHORITY OF ABŪ HURAYRAH.

43

A man who decides to perform Ḥajj should act with promptness, for he may fall sick, or his mount may get lost, or a need may arise that becomes an obstacle.

ḤADĪTH OF IBN MĀJAH ON THE AUTHORITY OF ʿABDULLĀH IBN AL-ʿABBĀS.

44

God's blessings are for everyone, but a strong believer is better than a weak one. Wish for things which are beneficial to you, and in this, seek God's help. Do not lose heart. If you are visited by misfortune, do not say, 'If I had done this or that, it could have been averted.' Because 'if' opens the door to Satan.

ḤADĪTH OF IBN MĀJAH, ON THE AUTHORITY OF ABŪ HURAYRAH.

45

Young man, (the Prophet said to
'Abdullāh ibn-al-'Abbās)
hear some words of advice:
Be mindful of God
and God will protect you.
Be mindful of God and
you will find Him before you.
If you ask, ask of God; if you seek help,
seek help of God. Know that if all
the people were to gather together
to give you the benefit of anything,
it would be something that
God had already prescribed for you,
and that if they gathered together to harm
you with anything, this would only be as
God had already ordained.

HADĪTH OF AT-TIRMIDHĪ.

Umm Salamah (the Prophet's wife)
recounts an incident which took place
when the Prophet was at home with her.
He called out to the maid servant,
and when she failed to appear,
he showed signs of displeasure.
Then Umm Salamah peeped out through
the curtain and saw the maid playing.
The Prophet,
who was holding a *miswāk*
(a twig for cleaning the teeth) in his hand,
said to the maidservant,
'If I had had no fear of retribution
on judgement Day,
I would have hit you with this twig.'

AL-ADAB AL-MUFRAD BY IMĀM AL-BUKHĀRĪ.

On the Day of Judgment,
from amongst all those destined for Hell,
a particular man,
the richest man in the world,
will be brought forth and cast into Hell
for a moment. Then he will be taken out
and will be asked, 'O son of Adam,
have you ever known
the good things of life?
Have you ever seen comfortable days?'
And he will reply,
'By God, O Lord, never.'
Then from amongst all those destined
for Paradise, one who has suffered
the most in the world will be
brought forth and will be allowed
to enter Paradise for a moment.
Then he will be taken out and asked,
'O son of Adam, have you ever seen

suffering? Have you ever experienced hardship in your life?'
He will reply, 'By God, no.
I have never suffered. I have never undergone hardship.'*

HADĪTH OF MUSLIM
ON THE AUTHORITY OF ANAS IBN MĀLIK.

* THAT IS, JUST ONE MOMENT IN HELL WOULD SUFFICE TO MAKE AN EVIL PERSON FORGET ALL THE ENJOYMENT HE MAY HAVE HAD IN LIFE, WHILE THE MERE SIGHT OF PARADISE WOULD BE ENOUGH TO MAKE A RIGHTEOUS MAN FORGET ALL THE SUFFERING HE MAY HAVE EXPERIENCED IN THE LIFE OF THIS WORLD.

48

According to Mu'ādh ibn Jabal, when the Prophet appointed him governor of Yemen, he said, 'Abstain from luxuries, for those who live luxurious lives are not servants of God.'

HADĪTH OF AHMAD IBN HANBAL.

49

A man who acquires a stretch of land
by tyranny will be made to wear a yoke
made of seven earths around his neck
on the Day of Judgment.

HADĪTH OF AL-BUKHĀRĪ AND MUSLIM
ON THE AUTHORITY OF SAʿĪD IBN ZAYD.

50

A man may speak of God's pleasure
without giving it much importance
and yet be raised in status by his Creator.
A man may say something which is
abhorrent to God, without attaching any
importance to it, and it may sweep him
straight into Hell.

ḤADĪTH OF AL-BUKHĀRĪ
ON THE AUTHORITY OF ABŪ HURAYRAH.

51

'A man who has as much as an iota of arrogance in his heart will not enter Paradise.' Hearing these words of the Prophet, a man asked, 'What if a man likes to dress in good clothes and wear good shoes?' The Prophet said, 'God himself possesses elegance. And He likes elegance. This has nothing to do with arrogance. A man is arrogant when he refuses to accept the truth and considers others to be inferior.'

HADĪTH OF MUSLIM
ON THE AUTHORITY OF ·ABDULLĀH IBN MAS·ŪD.

52

God accepts the repentance of a man right to his last gasp, before he dies.

HADĪTH OF AT-TIRMIDHĪ ON THE AUTHORITY OF
·ABDULLĀH IBN ·UMAR.

53

Abū Dharr al-Ghifārī, who went to
the Prophet for advice, was given
this counsel: 'Fear God,
for He is the one Who sets right all that
concerns you. Read the Qur'ān
and keep remembering God.
For then you will be remembered in the
heavens. And that will be a light
for you on the earth.'

ḤADĪTH OF AḤMAD IBN ḤANBAL.

54

'The heart becomes rusted like iron in water.'
When asked how to banish this corrosion,
the Prophet replied, 'Remember death fre-
quently and recite the Qur'ān.'

ḤADĪTH OF AN-NASĀ'Ī ON THE AUTHORITY OF
'ABDULLAH IBN 'UMAR.

According to Abū Hurayrah,
the Prophet recited a verse from
the Qur'ān about the Day the earth
would give its account.
Then he asked, 'Do you know what this
account will be?' His listeners replied,
'God and His Messenger know better.'
'The account the earth will give,'
said the Prophet, 'is the witness
it will bear to
the deeds and misdeeds all men
and women have committed
throughout its length and breadth,
and to the exact moments of their
commission. That is what the earth's
account will be.'

ḤADĪTH OF AT-TIRMIDHĪ.

Following the rule of abstinence from
worldly things does not mean that what is
normally permitted becomes prohibited
or that wealth should be allowed to go to
waste. On the contrary, such abstinence
means that you should place greater reliance
on what God intends for you than on what
you have in hand yourself And when misfortune strikes, you should relish its continuance
for the reward this will bring.

ḤADĪTH OF AT-TIRMIDHĪ
ON THE AUTHORITY OF ABŪ DHARR AL-GHIFĀRĪ.

57

Anyone who unjustly flogs his servant
will be punished on the Day of Judgment.

ḤADĪTH OF AT-TABARĀNĪ
ON THE AUTHORITY OF ABŪ HURAYRAH.

58

Love for the life of this world is damaging
to the life of the Hereafter.
Anyone who values the life of the Hereafter
will be indifferent to the life of this world.
Therefore, prefer that which is eternal to
that which is ephemeral.

HADĪTH OF AHMAD IBN HANBAL
ON THE AUTHORITY OF ABŪ MŪSĀ AL-ASH·ARĪ.

59

Wise is he who controls his desires
and prepares for the life which starts after
death. And cast down is he who lives
for the love of this world and has
false expectations from God.

HADĪTH OF AT-TIRMIDHĪ
ON THE AUTHORITY OF SHADDĀD IBN AUS.

60

On the Day of Judgment the rightful
will be given their due. So much so that
a goat with horns will be avenged
for the goat without horns.*

ḤADĪTH OF MUSLIM AND AT-TIRMIDHĪ
ON THE AUTHORITY OF ABŪ HURAYRAH.

* THAT IS, A PERSON WHO IS AS INSIGNIFICANT
AS A GOAT WITHOUT HORNS WILL ALSO
RECEIVE HIS DUE ON THAT DAY.

61

The lightest punishment for those in
Hell will be two sparks under both feet.
So searing will be their effect that the brain
will begin to boil like a vessel
on the fireplace.

ḤADĪTH OF AL-BUKHĀRĪ AND MUSLIM
ON THE AUTHORITY OF NUʿMĀN IBN BASHĪR.

62

On the Day of Judgment,
no step shall a man stir until he has
answered questions on five aspects
of his wordly existence: his life and
how he spent it; his knowledge and
what use he has made of it; his wealth,
how he acquired it and how he has spent it;
and his body and how he has utilized it.

ḤADĪTH OF AT-TIRMIDHĪ
ON THE AUTHORITY OF ABŪ HURAYRAH.

63

The cautious man travels early in the morning. And the early morning traveller reaches
his destination. Pay heed. God's reward is
peerless. Pay heed. God's reward is Paradise.

ḤADĪTH OF AT-TIRMIDHĪ
ON THE AUTHORITY OF ABŪ HURAYRAH.

64

The man who enters Paradise will live in eternal blessedness. He will never be needy. Neither will his clothes wear out, nor will he lose his youth. Paradise has everything–things which have never been seen or heard of, and which are quite beyond human imagination.

HADĪTH OF MUSLIM
ON THE AUTHORITY OF ABŪ HURAYRAH.

65

According to Asmā' bint Abū Bakr, the Prophet once stood up and delivered a sermon in which he spoke of the trials that a man would be subjected to beyond the grave. When he delivered this discourse, the believers wept bitterly.

HADĪTH OF AL-BUKHĀRĪ

When those destined for Paradise
enter it, to each a herald will cry:
'Now you will enjoy good health forever.
You will never fall ill.
You will retain your youth forever.
You will never grow old.
You will be prosperous forever.
You will never be needy.
This is the essence of
God's promise to you.
Then a cry will go up:
'This is the Paradise
you were promised.
You have been made its inheritor
in return
for your good deeds' (7:43).

HADĪTH OF MUSLIM AND AT-TIRMIDHĪ
ON THE AUTHORITY OF ABŪ HURAYRAH.

A man thus addressed the Prophet:
'O Messenger of God,
who rightfully deserves the
best treatment from me?'
'Your mother,'
the Prophet said.
'Then who?' the man asked again.
'Your mother,'
replied the Prophet.
'Then who?'
asked the man once again.
'Your mother,' said the Prophet.
The man asked once more,
'Then who?'
'Your father,'
said the noble Prophet.

HADĪTH OF AL-BUKHĀRĪ AND MUSLIM
ON THE AUTHORITY OF ABŪ HURAYRAH.

68

The Prophet once exclaimed,
'Shame on him!
Shame on him!
Shame on him!'
When asked who the man in
question
was, the prophet replied,
'He is one who had both or
one of his parents with
him in their old age,
yet he failed to
enter Paradise.'

ḤADĪTH OF MUSLIM
ON THE AUTHORITY OF ABŪ HURAYRAH.

69

Abū Usayd as-Saʿīdī tells of how they
were once with the Prophet
when a man from the Banu Salmah
arrived in their midst.
Addressing the Prophet, he asked,
'O Messenger of God,
Are there any outstanding debts
which I have to repay after my parents'
deaths?' The Prophet, replied,
'Yes, pray for them and
seek forgiveness for them.
And fulfill their obligations now that
they are gone. And treat their relations
with kindness.
And respect their friends.'

ḤADĪTH OF ABŪ DĀWŪD.

70

A man who treats his relatives
well in order to return their
good treatment of him shows
no real love for them. The man
who really shows love for his relatives
is one who treats them well despite
their being unkind to him.

ḤADĪTH OF AL-BUKHĀRĪ
ON THE AUTHORITY OF ʿABDULLAH IBN ʿUMAR

71

He who satiates himself,
while his immediate neighbours go hungry,
is not a true believer.

ḤADĪTH OF AḤMAD IBN ḤANBAL
ON THE AUTHORITY OF ʿABDULLĀH IBN ʿABBĀS.

72

Asma' bint Abū Bakr related how her
foster Mother, a believer in
polytheism (*shirk*), had come to her during
the period of the treaty of al-Hudaybiyyah.
Concerned that her foster Brother was a
polytheist, she addressed the Prophet,
'O Messenger of God, my idolatrous (*mushrik*)
mother has come to me and she wants something from me. Should I give it to her?' 'Yes.
Treat her well,' replied the Prophet.

ḤADĪTH OF AL-BUKHĀRĪ AND MUSLIM.

73

A man who has two wives, but does not give
them equal treatment, will find half his
body lost on the Day of Judgment.

ḤADĪTH OF AT-TIRMIDHĪ.
ON THE AUTHORITY OF ABŪ HURAYRAH.

74

When a man dies, nothing lives on
after him, except for three things:
ṣadaqah jāriyah (continuing charity),*
knowledge which can benefit others, or
virtuous offspring who will pray for him.

ḤADĪTH OF MUSLIM ON
THE AUTHORITY OF ABŪ HURAYRAH.

* THAT IS, HIS CHARITY, THE BENEFIT OF WHICH
CONTINUES EVEN AFTER THE DONOR HAS PASSED
AWAY, SUCH AS THE BUILDING OF A BRIDGE OR A
HOSPITAL, OR THE DIGGING OF A WELL.

75

A believer should never loathe a believing
wife. If one quality in her does not find
favour with her husband, some other
quality will be to his liking.

ḤADĪTH OF MUSLIM
ON THE AUTHORITY OF ABŪ HURAYRAH.

A man once went to the Prophet with a
grievance against his relatives.
'O Messenger of God,'
he said,
'I have some relatives whom I treat with
kindness. Yet they show me no kindness.
I treat them well and they treat me badly.
I show them forbearance
and they treat me with brutality.'
The Prophet replied,
'If you are as you say,
you are then it is as if,
you have smeared their faces with dust.
And you will always have God's help
against them so long as you continue
to be well-behaved towards them.'

HADĪTH OF MUSLIM
ON THE AUTHORITY OF ABŪ HURAYRAH.

77

When the Prophet Muhammad ﷺ was
asked who was the best of all women,
he replied, 'The woman whose husband
feels pleased to see her,
who obeys when her husband commands,
and who does not take a stand about her
or her wealth which is
displeasing to her husband.'

ḤADĪTH OF AN-NASĀʾĪ
ON THE AUTHORITY OF ABŪ HURAYRAH.

78

When a man spends on his family members
with the intention of seeking God's pleasure,
then his spending becomes an act of charity.

ḤADĪTH OF AL-BUKHĀRĪ AND MUSLIM
ON THE AUTHORITY OF ABŪ MASʿŪD.

A person once said to the Prophet,
'O Messenger of God, a certain woman
is said to offer ṣalāt (prayers),
observe fasts and give alms generously,
but she hurts her neighbours
by the way she speaks.'
The Prophet replied,
'She will go to Hell.'
Then the man said, 'O Messenger of God,
a certain other woman says
fewer prayers,
keeps fewer fasts voluntarily
and offers little in the way of alms.
She only gives a few pieces of cheese.
But she never hurts her neighbours with her
tongue.' The Prophet replied,
'She will enter Paradise.'

ḤADĪTH OF AḤMAD IBN ḤANBAL
ON THE AUTHORITY OF ABŪ HURAYRAH

80

When the Prophet was asked by
'Ā'ishah to which of two neighbours
she should send a gift, he replied,
'To the one whose door is closer to your own.'

HADĪTH OF AL-BUKHARĪ.

81

The Prophet once exclaimed,
'By God, he is not a believer!
By God, he is not a believer!
By God, he is not a believer!'
The people asked, 'O Messenger of God,
who?' 'The man whose excesses prevent his
neighbour from living in peace,'
replied the noble Prophet.

HADĪTH OF AL-BUKHARĪ.
ON THE AUTHORITY OF ABŪ HURAYRAH.

82

A believer is a mirror to another believer.
A believer is a brother to another believer.
He saves him from losses.
He safeguards his interests in his absence.

HADĪTH OF ABŪ DĀWŪD
ON THE AUTHORITY OF ABŪ HURAYRAH.

83

According to Anas ibn Mālik,
the Prophet said to him,
'O my son, if you can act in such a way that
you spend your mornings and your evenings
without wishing anyone ill, then that is how
you should always act.' Then he added,
'O my son, this is my way. And anyone who
loves my ways, loves me. And anyone who
loves me will live with me in Paradise.'

HADĪTH OF MUSLIM.

Each one of you is a shepherd.
And each one of you will be asked
about your flock. A ruler also is a shepherd
and he will be asked about his flock.
And every man is a shepherd to his family.
And a woman is the custodian to her
husband's house and his children.
Thus each one of you is a shepherd, and each
one will be asked about his flock.

HADĪTH OF AL-BUKHARĪ AND MUSLIM
ON THE AUTHORITY OF 'ABDULLĀH IBN 'UMAR.

85

You should visit the sick, feed the hungry
and set prisoners free.

HADĪTH OF AL-BUKHARĪ
ON THE AUTHORITY OF ABŪ MŪSĀ AL-ASH'ARĪ.

86

Whenever God makes a man responsible
for other people, whether in greater
or lesser numbers, he will be questioned
as to whether he ruled his charges
in accordance with God's decrees or not.
And that will not be all. God will question
him even about his family members.

ḤADĪTH OF AḤMAD IBN ḤANBAL
ON THE AUTHORITY OF 'ABDULLAH IBN 'UMAR.

87

If you show kindness to your servant
while employing him in some task,
this will weigh heavily in your favour
on the Day of Judgment.
That will be your reward.

ḤADĪTH OF 'AMR IBN HURAYTH.

88

The best person among you is the one
who treats his family members well.
And I am the best person for my family.

ḤADĪTH OF IBN MĀJAH
ON THE AUTHORITY OF 'ABDULLĀH IBN AL-
'ABBĀS.

89

When the Prophet was asked
which form of Islam was better,
he replied,
'To feed the people
and extend greetings
of peace to them–be they
of your acquaintance or not.'

ḤADĪTH OF AL-BUKHĀRĪ AND MUSLIM
ON THE AUTHORITY OF
'ABDULLĀH IBN 'AMR IBN AL-'ĀṢ.

90

On the Day of Judgment,
God will say,
'O son of Adam,
I was sick,
but you did not visit Me.'
The man will reply,
'O my Lord,
how could I visit You– the Lord of the
whole universe?' God will say,
'Did you not know that such and such
a man had fallen ill?
Yet you did not visit him.
Did you not know that
had you gone there to visit him,
you would have
found Me there with him?'

ḤADĪTH OF MUSLIM
ON THE AUTHORITY OF ABŪ HURAYRAH.

91

O Muslim women,
do not belittle the gift of any woman
in your neighbourhood, even if it
happens to be a goat's hoof.

ḤADĪTH OF AL-BUKHĀRĪ AND MUSLIM
ON THE AUTHORITY OF ABŪ HURAYRAH.

92

According to Anas ibn Mālik,
when God's Messenger said,
'Help your brother, irrespective of whether
he is the oppressor or the oppressed,'
a man said, 'O Messenger of God,
I can help the oppressed, but how can I help
the oppressor?' The Prophet replied, 'Stop him
from committing an act of oppression.
That in itself is a form of help.'

ḤADĪTH OF AL-BUKHĀRĪ AND MUSLIM.

93

According to 'Abdullāh ibn 'Umar, the
Prophet, addressing the people
on the occasion of the farewell pilgrimage,
exhorted them to listen carefully
to what he had to say:
'All Muslims are brothers.
They constitute one brotherhood.
Nothing belonging to one Muslim can
become legitimate property of another,
unless it has been freely and willingly given.
Do not, therefore, do injustice
to your own selves. O God,
have I conveyed your message?
Woe betide you. When I am gone,
do not become infidels
and start killing each other.'

ḤADĪTH OF AL-BUKHĀRĪ.

94

Do not marry women for their beauty.
It is possible that their beauty may destroy
them. Do not marry them for their wealth. It
is possible that their wealth may make them
rebellious. Instead, marry them on the basis
of their faith. And a black maid who is a
believer is much better for you.

ḤADĪTH OF IBN MĀJAH
ON THE AUTHORITY OF ʿABDULLAH
IBN ʿAMR IBN AL-ʿĀṢ.

95

The worst feast is the marriage feast to which
the rich are invited and the poor are not. And
anyone who does not accept an invitation
commits an act of disobedience, against God
and His Messenger.

ḤADĪTH OF AL-BUKHĀRĪ AND MUSLIM
ON THE AUTHORITY OF ABŪ HURAYRAH.

96

According to Jarīr ibn 'Abdullāh, when he
asked the Prophet about a man's gaze
falling inadvertently on a strange woman,
the Prophet replied,
'Turn your eyes away.'

HADĪTH OF MUSLIM.

97

O young people, those among you
who are able must enter into marriage.
For it helps to divert your attention from
women. And it is a safeguard against lust.
And those who cannot marry should observe
fasts, for fasting too is a safeguard.

HADĪTH OF AL-BUKHĀRĪ AND MUSLIM
ON THE AUTHORITY OF 'ABDULLĀH IBN MAS'ŪD.

98

There are four reasons for a man
to marry a woman:
her wealth;
her lineage;
her beauty;
her faith.
Woe betide you!
Only enter into marriage with one
who has faith.

ḤADĪTH OF AL-BUKHĀRĪ AND MUSLIM
ON THE AUTHORITY OF ABŪ HURAYRAH.

99

The best gift from a father to his child is
education and upbringing.

ḤADĪTH OF AT-TIRMIDHĪ
ON THE AUTHORITY OF SAʿĪD IBN AL-ʿAṢ.

100

The best dower is the easy one.

ḤADĪTH OF ABŪ DĀWŪD
ON THE AUTHORITY OF ŪQBAH IBN ʿĀMĪR.

101

Should I not tell you
what is the best charity? To spend on the
daughter who has been returned to you
(a divorced or widowed daughter),
when there is no one else to earn for her.

ḤADĪTH OF IBN MĀJAH
ON THE AUTHORITY OF SURAQA IBN MĀLIK.

102

According to ʿĀʾishah, once when
a child was brought to the Prophet,
he fondled him and said, 'These children
make cowards and misers of the parents. And
they are the flowers of the Almighty.'

ḤADĪTH OF IBN MĀJAH.

103

According to ʻAbdullāh ibn al-ʻAbbās,
the Prophet cursed
those men
who try to resemble women
and women
who try to resemble men.

ḤADĪTH OF AL-BUKHĀRĪ ABŪ DĀWŪD
AND AN-NASĀʼĪ.

104

On the Day of Judgement,
what will weigh most heavily in
favour of the believer will be his
good morals. God abhors those
who indulge in shameless talk
and use indecent language.

ḤADĪTH OF AT-TIRMIDHĪ
ON THE AUTHORITY OF ABŪʼD DARDĀ.

105

Save yourselves from envy.
For envy eats up virtue
as fire eats up Wood.

ḤADĪTH OF ABŪ DĀWŪD
ON THE AUTHORITY OF ABŪ HURAYRAH.

106

It is not proper for a man
to keep away from his brother
for more than three days,
and then when they meet to
turn their faces, away from each other.
The better of the two is the one
who greets the other first.

ḤADĪTH OF AL-BUKHĀRĪ AND MUSLIM
ON THE AUTHORITY OF ABŪ AYYŪB AL-ANṢĀRĪ.

107

An honest and trustworthy merchant
(in the world hereafter)
will be with the Prophets,
the truthful and the martyrs.

ḤADĪTH OF AT-TIRMIDHĪ
ON THE AUTHORITY OF ABŪ SAʿĪD AL-KHUDRĪ.

108

According to Abū Mūsā al-Ashʿarī,
the Prophet said,
'Believers are like the different parts
of a building, each one supporting the other.'
Then he demonstrated what he meant by
interlocking his fingers.

ḤADĪTH OF AL-BUKHĀRĪ AND MUSLIM.

109

How evil is the man who hoards
essential supplies! If God wills it that the
prices of merchandise fall,
that makes him unhappy.
But if the prices rise,
that makes him happy.

HADĪTH OF AL-BAYHAQĪ
ON THE AUTHORITY OF MU·ĀDH.

110

You will observe that the believers are
like the parts of the body in relation to
each other in matters of kindness,
love and affection. When one part of the
body is afflicted, the entire body feels it;
there is loss of sleep and a fever develops.

HADĪTH OF AL-BUKHĀRĪ AND MUSLIM
ON THE AUTHORITY OF NU·MĀN IBN BASHĪR.

111

To earn through labour
is the best way to earn, provided
the work is done with sincerity.

HADĪTH OF AHMAD IBN HANBAL
ON THE AUTHORITY OF ABŪ HURAYRAH.

112

It is obligatory for a Muslim to pay
heed to his ruler and obey him,
whether he likes him or not,
as long as the ruler does not order him to
commit a sin. If he orders him to sin,
then he is not to pay heed to him
or obey him.

HADĪTH OF AL-BUKHĀRĪ AND MUSLIM
ON THE AUTHORITY OF ABDULLĀH IBN 'UMAR.

113

Muslims are brothers.
When one Muslim sells something to another,
it is his duty to inform the other
of any defect in the merchandise.

ḤADĪTH OF IBN MĀJAH
ON THE AUTHORITY OF ʿUQBAH IBN ʿĀMIR.

114

Avoid falling under suspicion.
For suspicion does the worst damage.
Do not inquire into the lives of others.
Do not pry.
Do not exaggerate what others say.
Bear each other no malice, and
do not hurt each others' interests.
And, by being brothers to each other
become the servants of God.

ḤADĪTH OF MUSLIM
ON THE AUTHORITY OF ABŪ HURAYRAH

115

The best sustenance is that which
you earn by your own industry.
The Prophet Dāwūd (David) used to earn his
sustenance with his own hands.

HADĪTH OF AL-BUKHĀRĪ
ON THE AUTHORITY OF MIQDAM IBN MA·DIKARIB.

116

According to Suhayl when
God's Messenger passed by a camel and
noticed that it had become so thin,
that its back and its stomach seemed to be
touching, he said, 'Fear God when dealing
with these beasts. Mount them when
they are in good condition,
and leave them in that same state.'

HADĪTH OF ABŪ DĀWŪD.

117

A merchant who hoards goods in order to
raise their price is a sinner.

ḤADĪTH OF MUSLIM
ON THE AUTHORITY OF MAʿMAR.

118

According to Rāfiʿ ibn Khadīj,
when the Prophet was asked which was the
best kind of earning, he replied,
'That for which a man works with his hands.
And honest trading.'

ḤADĪTH OF AḤMAD IBN ḤANBAL.

119

A time will come when people will no longer
care about whether their wealth has been
lawfully or unlawfully acquired.

ḤADĪTH OF AL-BUKHĀRĪ
ON THE AUTHORITY OF ABŪ HURAYRAH.

120

It is not just for a man to sell
his merchandise without disclosing
its defects. It is proper for the
vendor to tell the buyer
of any defects of which he is aware.

ḤADĪTH OF AḤMAD IBN ḤANBAL
ON THE AUTHORITY OF WATHILAH.

121

The trader who does not hoard
essential supplies receives
His sustenance, while the hoarder
of essential supplies is cursed.

ḤADĪTH OF IBN MĀJAH AND AD-DĀRIMĪ
ON THE AUTHORITY OF ʿUMAR IBN AL-KHAṬṬAB.

122

Allah will show compassion
to those who show kindness while
buying and selling, and recovering debts.

ḤADĪTH OF AL-BUKHĀRĪ
ON THE AUTHORITY OF JĀBIR.

123

One who denies an heir his legacy
will be denied the legacy of Paradise
by the Almighty.

ḤADĪTH OF IBN MĀJAH
ON THE AUTHORITY OF ANAS IBN MĀLIK.

124

One who makes sacrifices
for the sake of God will have all his sins
pardoned, except for his debts.

ḤADĪTH OF MUSLIM
ON THE AUTHORITY OF ʿABDULLAH IBN ʿUMAR.

125

Pay the labourer his wages even
before his sweat dries up.

ḤADĪTH OF IBN MĀJAH
ON THE AUTHORITY OF ʿABDULLĀH IBN ʿUMAR.

126

There was a man who used to give
loans to poor people. When his assistant had
to go to them to recover, the loans,
he would urge him to be forgiving to those
who were not able to
pay back his loans with ease,
believing that, in that way,
perhaps **God** would show him forgiveness.
When that man came face to face with the
Almighty, He forgave him.

ḤADĪTH OF AL-BUKHĀRĪ AND MUSLIM
ON THE AUTHORITY OF ABŪ HURAYRAH.

127

If a man commits something to your care,
be sure to return it to him.
Never betray anyone's trust,
not even if the person concerned
has failed to stand by his
commitments to you.

ḤADĪTH OF AT-TIRMIDHĪ
ON THE AUTHORITY OF ABŪ HURAYRAH.

128

Save yourself from the curse of
an oppressed person, who seeks his rights
from God,
for God never denies
the righteous their rights.

ḤADĪTH OF AL-BAYHAQĪ
ON THE AUTHORITY OF ʿALĪ IBN ABĪ ṬĀLIB.

129

if a Muslim farms the land or plants a tree,
and then a bird, a beast or a man
eats something from it, he receives
in return the reward of a charity.

ḤADĪTH OF MUSLIM
ON THE AUTHORITY OF ANAS IBN MĀLIK.

130

What is lawful and what is forbidden
are both quite clear. But between them are
matters which are not clear. A man who
avoids the unclear will be even more careful
to avoid an open sin. But it is feared that a
man who does not baulk at unclear sins
will indulge even in open sin. And sin is like
a grazing ground forbidden by God.
A beast that passes by it risks the chance of
straying into it.

ḤADĪTH OF AL-BUKHĀRĪ AND MUSLIM
ON THE AUTHORITY OF NU'MĀN IBN BASHĪR.

131

On the Day of Judgment,
God will not even look at a man who,
in a show of arrogance, lets his clothes sweep
the ground. Abū Bakr said,
'The cloth which I have worn around my
waist trails no matter what I do.'
To this the Prophet said, 'You are not one of
those who do it out of arrogance.'

HADĪTH OF AL-BUKHĀRĪ
ON THE AUTHORITY OF ʿABDULLĀH IBN ʿUMAR.

132

One who walks with a tyrant,
in the full knowledge that he is a tyrant,
in order to strengthen him, is such as has
already left the fold of Islam.

HADĪTH OF AL-BAYHAQĪ
ON THE AUTHORITY OF AUS IBN SHURAḤABĪL.

133

A man who borrows things,
with the intention of returning them,
has them returned on his behalf by the
Almighty. A man who borrows things,
with no intention of returning them,
has such possessions destroyed
by the Almighty.

ḤADĪTH OF- AL-BUKHĀRĪ
ON THE AUTHORITY OF ABŪ HURAYRAH.

134

Anger is the devil, and the devil has been
created from fire. And fire is extinguished
by water, therefore, when
any of you feel angry,
you should perform your ablutions.

ḤADĪTH OF ABŪ DĀWŪD
ON THE AUTHORITY OF ʿATIYAH SAʿDĪ.

135

When any of you feel angry,
you should sit down if you are standing.
And if your anger passes off with this,
well and good.
If not, you should lie down.

ḤADĪTH OF ABŪ DĀWŪD
ON THE AUTHORITY OF ABŪ DHARR AL-GHIFĀRĪ.

136

When a man tells you something in
confidence, you must not betray his trust.

ḤADĪTH OF ABŪ DĀWŪD
ON THE AUTHORITY OF JĀBIR IBN 'ABDULLĀH.

137

On the Day of Judgment, the tyrant's
own tyranny will descend upon him
in the form of darkness.

ḤADĪTH OF AL-BUKHĀRĪ AND MUSLIM
ON THE AUTHORITY OF 'ABDULLĀH IBN 'UMAR.

138

When there are three of you,
one should not be left out
while the other two share a secret,
for this will cause him grief.

HADĪTH OF AHMAD IBN HANBAL
ON THE AUTHORITY OF 'ABDULLĀH IBN 'UMAR.

139

Whosoever of you sees an evil action,
let him change it with his hand;
and if he is not able to do so,
then with his tongue;
and if he is not able to do so,
then with his heart, for that is the minimum
that is desirable from a believer.

HADĪTH OF AN-NASĀ'Ī
ON THE AUTHORITY OF ABŪ SA'ĪD AL-KHUDRĪ.

140

No one should have to ask another
to vacate his seat for him. Room should be
made for him without his asking.

ḤADĪTH OF AḤMAD
ON THE AUTHORITY OF 'ABDULLĀH IBN 'UMAR.

141

It is not proper for a man to sit
between two men and thus separate them,
without seeking their permission.

ḤADĪTH OF ABŪ DĀWŪD AND
AT-TIRMIDHĪ ON THE AUTHORITY OF 'AMR IBN
SHU'AYB.

142

Those who take bribes and those who give
bribes are cursed by God.

ḤADĪTH OF AL-BUKHĀRĪ AND MUSLIM
ON THE AUTHORITY OF
'ABDULLĀH IBN 'AMR IBN AL-'ĀṢ.

By his own account,
'Amr ibn 'Abasah met the Prophet
in Mecca in the early days
of his prophethood,
and asked him, 'What are you?'
He replied, 'I am a Prophet.'
'Amr then asked, 'What is a Prophet?'
He replied, 'I have been sent by God.'
'What has God sent you with?'
'Amr asked. 'With the commandment
to destroy idols and
to treat one's relatives with kindness;
to believe in one God
and
not to treat
anyone as His partner,'
replied the Prophet.

HADĪTH OF MUSLIM.

144

Three things are part of the
good morals of a believer.
When he is overcome by anger,
his anger should not drive him to falsehood.
When he is happy,
his happiness should not take him
beyond the bounds of what is right.
When he has power, he should not stake a
claim to something which is not his.

ḤADĪTH OF AṬ-ṬABARĀNĪ
ON THE AUTHORITY OF ANAS IBN MĀLIK.

145

The way to atone for slander is to
pray for the forgiveness of the person
whom you have slandered. Say, 'O God,
forgive me as well as him.'

ḤADĪTH OF AL-JAMI' AṢ-ṢAGHĪR
ON THE AUTHORITY OF ANAS IBN MĀLIK.

146

Explaining verse 41:34 of the Qur'ān,
'Abdullāh ibn 'Abbās said that
those who exercised self-restraint
when angry, or when confronted by mischief,
would be protected by God.
He would force their enemies
to bow down before them
as if they were His dear friends.

HADĪTH OF AL-BUKHĀRĪ.

147

Whenever a believer is striken
with any hardship, or pain, or anxiety,
or sorrow, or harm, or distress–even if it
be a thorn that has hurt him–Allah redeems
thereby some of his failings.

HADĪTH OF AL-BUKHĀRĪ AND MUSLIM.

148

Anas ibn Mālik relates that
as he was walking with the Prophet,
who happened to have a thick-bordered
Najrānī *burd* (sheet)
around his shoulders,
a Bedouin came up to him and tugged at it.
'I saw that it had left a mark on his neck.
Then the Bedouin said,
"O Muḥammad, order some of the
wealth of God which you have in your
possession to be given to me."
The Prophet looked at him and smiled,
then he gave orders
for something to be given to him.'

HADĪTH OF AL-BUKHĀRĪ AND MUSLIM.

149

A bedouin once urinated
in the Prophet's Mosque,
and people got up to punish him.
The Prophet said, 'Leave him alone, and
throw a bucket of water over his urine.
You are here to make things easy,
not to make things difficult.'

ḤADĪTH OF AL-BUKHĀRĪ
ON THE AUTHORITY OF ABŪ HURAYRAH.

150

According to 'Ā'ishah,
the Prophet used to cobble his shoes,
stitch his clothes and do the kind of
housework that is done in all homes.
He was a human being
just like anybody else. He used to milk his
goat and do sundry other chores himself.

ḤADĪTH OF AT-TIRMIDHĪ.

151

According to 'Ā'ishah,
the Prophet never gave others tasks which
were beyond their capabilities.

HADĪTH OF AL-BUKHĀRĪ.

152

According to 'Abdullāh ibn 'Amr ibn al-'Āṣ,
the Prophet was never seen to eat while
reclining on a pillow.
And no one had seen even two men walking
behind him at any time.

HADĪTH OF ABŪ DĀWŪD.

153

'Ā'ishah said that she had never seen the
Prophet show off his palate.
He used just to smile.

HADĪTH OF AL-BUKHĀRĪ AND MUSLIM.

154

Sā'ib has thus recorded his
commendation of the Prophet;
'In the period of Ignorance
(i.e. before Islam) when you were
my partner in business,
you were the finest of all partners.
You never deceived me. Neither did you
quarrel with me.'

HADĪTH OF ABŪ DĀWŪD.

155

According to Ya'ala when he asked
Umm Salamah how the Prophet recited
the Qur'ān, she replied,
'The Prophet used to recite the Qur'ān
with great clarity.
Each word could be heard distinctly.'

HADĪTH OF AT-TIRMIDHĪ.

156

According to Jābir,
the Prophet never said 'no' to any request.

ḤADĪTH OF AL-BUKHĀRĪ AND MUSLIM.

157

'Abdullāh ibn Mas'ūd told how during
the battle of Badr, one camel was shared by
three men, namely Abū Lubabah,
'Alī ibn Abī Ṭālib, and the Prophet.
When it was the Prophet's turn to walk,
the other two would say to him,
'Mount the camel. We will walk in your
place.' The Prophet would reply,
'Neither of you is stronger than I am,
nor am I less eager for rewards than you.'

ḤADĪTH OF AHMAD IBN ḤANBAL.

158

Abū Hurayrah relates how
the Prophet never criticised food.
'If he liked it, he ate it. If he did not,
he just left it.'

HADĪTH OF AL-BUKHĀRĪ AND MUSLIM.

159

According to 'Abdullāh ibn Mas'ūd, the
Prophet said that none of his
Companions should complain to him of
another. 'I would like to come to you
with a clear heart.'

HADĪTH OF ABŪ DĀWŪD.

160

According to 'Ā'ishah, the Prophet held that
cleaning the teeth helped in maintaining oral
hygiene. 'And,' said the Prophet, 'it gives
pleasure to the Lord.'

HADĪTH OF AHMAD IBN HANBAL AND AN-NASĀ'Ī.

161

Verily, God Almighty, and His angels,
and those who inhabit the heavens,
even the ants in their holes
and the fishes in their waters,
bless the good teachers of mankind.

ḤADĪTH OF AT-TIRMIDHĪ
ON THE AUTHORITY OF ABŪ UMĀMAH.

162

You will not enter Paradise unless
you have faith, and you cannot be
one of the faithful unless you love each other.
Should I not tell you things which,
if followed, will create love among you?
One is to observe the practice of
greeting each other.

ḤADĪTH OF MUSLIM
ON THE AUTHORITY OF ABŪ HURAYRAH.

163

According to 'Abdullāh ibn al-'Abbās,
the Prophet forbade the staging
of fights between animals.

ḤADĪTH OF AT-TIRMIDHĪ.

164

According to 'Abdullāh ibn 'Umar,
the Prophet forbade not only indulgence
in slander and backbiting,
but even listening to such talk

MISHKĀT AL-MAṢĀBĪḤ.

165

When a man makes a promise with the
intention of fulfilling it, but for some valid
reason is unable to do so,
he does not thereby commit a sin.

ḤADĪTH OF ABŪ DĀWŪD
ON THE AUTHORITY OF ZAYD IBN ARQAM.

166

According to Khuraym ibn Fatik,
the Prophet rose after the completion
of his morning prayer and said,
'The giving of false evidence is like
committing idolatry.' He repeated this three
times. Then he recited this passage of the
Qur'ān: 'Shun the loathsome evil of
idolatrous beliefs and practices;
and shun every word that is untrue.
Dedicate yourselves to God and serve none
besides Him' (22:30-31).

ḤADĪTH OF ABŪ DĀWŪD.

167

'The man who indulges in backbiting
will not enter Paradise!'

ḤADĪTH OF BUKHĀRĪ
ON THE AUTHORITY OF ABŪ HURAYRAH.

168

A man once asked the Prophet if bigotry
was to love one's tribe.
'No,' replied the Prophet.
'Bigotry is to help your tribe
to tyrannise others.'

ḤADĪTH OF IBN MĀJAH ON THE
AUTHORITY OF 'UBADAH IBN KATHĪR ASH-SHĀMĪ.

169

He who preaches bigotry is not one of us.
And not being one of us,
he may go ahead and fight in the cause
of bigotry. He who dies for such a
cause is not one of us either.

ḤADĪTH OF ABŪ DĀWŪD
ON THE AUTHORITY OF JUBAYR IBN MUṬ·IM.

According to Abū Hurayrah,
the Prophet once asked his listners
if they knew what slander was,
to which they replied that
God and His Messenger knew better.
The Prophet then explained that
slander meant speaking of one's brother
in a manner that was hurtful to him.
He was then asked, what if one's brother was
actually at fault. The Prophet replied that,
if he was at fault,
then what was said against him
was just backbiting and,
if he was not,
it was calumny.

HADĪTH OF MUSLIM
ON THE AUTHORITY OF ABŪ HURAYRAH.

171

'On the Day of Judgment, you will
discover the worst man to be the one
who had two faces.'

HADĪTH OF AL-BUKHĀRĪ AND MUSLIM
ON THE AUTHORITY OF ABŪ HURAYRAH.

172

'Abdullāh said that it was not proper
to tell lies either in serious or in light vein.
Neither was it proper
to make promises
to one's children
and then not fulfill them.

AL-ADAB AL-MUFRAD
BY IMĀM AL-BUKHĀRĪ

173

There are four characteristics
which together make a person
a complete hypocrite.
The taint of hypocrisy will, attach to the
trustee who breaks his trust, to the speaker
who tells untruths, to the maker of promises
who fails to keep them and to the man who
uses foul language when in disagreement with
others. This taint will remain unless the
wrongdoer mends his ways.

ḤADĪTH OF AL-BUKHĀRĪ AND MUSLIM
ON THE AUTHORITY OF ʿABDULLĀH IBN ʿAMR IBN
AL-ʿĀS.

174

When three men travel together,
they should make one of them their leader.

ḤADĪTH OF ABŪ DĀWŪD
ON THE AUTHORITY OF ABŪ SAʿĪD AL-KHUDRI.

175

Do not quarrel with your brother.
Do not ridicule him.
You should refrain from
making a promise
and then going back on it.

ḤADĪTH OF AT-TIRMIDHĪ
ON THE AUTHORITY OF ABDULLĀH IBN AL-ʿABBĀS.

176

A man who helps his people for an unjust
cause can be compared with a man,
who catches hold of the tail of a camel
which is failing into a well.

ḤADĪTH OF ABŪ DĀWŪD
ON THE AUTHORITY OF ʿABDULLĀH IBN MASʿŪD

177

It is ruinous for a man to tell lies so that
others may laugh.
It is ruinous for him.
It is ruinous for him.

ḤADĪTH OF AT-TIRMIDHĪ
ON THE AUTHORITY OF BAHZ IBN ḤAKĪM.

178

Do not rejoice in the misfortunes of your
brother. For God may show him compassion,
but create difficulties for you.

ḤADĪTH OF AT-TIRMIDHĪ
ON THE AUTHORITY OF WATHILAH.

179

The most perfect of believers, in point of
faith, is he who is the best in manners.

ḤADĪTH OF ABŪ DĀWŪD
ON THE AUTHORITY OF ABŪ HURAYRAH.

180

Even if a group of people in a jungle
number only three, it is still incumbent
upon them to choose a leader.

ḤADĪTH OF ABŪ DĀWŪD
ON THE AUTHORITY OF ʿABDULLĀH IBN ʿAMR

181

None of you (truly) believes,
until he wishes for his brother
what he wishes for himself.

ḤADĪTH OF BUKHĀRĪ
ON THE AUTHORITY OF ANAS IBN MĀLIK.

182

Calling God in personal prayer
is worship.

ḤADĪTH OF ABŪ DĀWŪD AND AT-TIRMIDHĪ
ON THE AUTHORITY OF NUʿMĀN IBN BASHĪR.

183

O God,
only You can change our hearts.
We beseech You to do so,
so that we may submit to You.

ḤADĪTH OF MUSLIM ON THE
AUTHORITY OF ʿABDULLĀH IBN ʿAMR IBN AL-ʿĀṢ.

184

According to Abū Bakr aṣ-Ṣiddiq,
when he asked the Prophet to tell him
of some invocations which he could recite
in his prayers, the Prophet said,
'Say, God, I have been an oppressor to myself.
And there is no one but You who can forgive
my sins. Therefore forgive me in
Your generosity. And show me
compassion. Verily, You are
Forgiving and Compassionate.'

ḤADĪTH OF AT-TIRMIDHĪ AND MUSLIM.

185

According to Mu'ādh,
the Prophet took his hand in his own
and said, 'O Mu'ādh, by God, I love You.'
Then he said, 'I give you this counsel:
after each prayer, you must not omit to say,
'O God, help me to remember You, and thank
You, and worship You with devotion.''

ḤADĪTH OF ABŪ DĀWŪD AND AN-NASĀ'Ī.

186

Ṭāriq ibn Ahyam relates that when anyone
entered the fold of Islam, the Prophet would
teach him to pray. Then he would instruct
him how to invoke his Maker in these words:
'O God, forgive me and have mercy on me.
Give me prosperity and sustenance.'

ḤADĪTH OF MUSLIM.

187

God has given utterance to these words:
'We are with Our servant whenever
he remembers Us;
when his lips are busy for Us.'

ḤADĪTH OF BUKHĀRĪ
ON THE AUTHORITY OF ABŪ HURAYRAH.

188

O God, I have obtained one promise
from You. And on no account will You go
against it. After all, I am a human being.
(If ever) I have harmed a Muslim,
or have spoken ill of him, or cursed him,
or flogged him, then in compensation
for all this,
give him Your blessings,
Your purity and Your nearness.

ḤADĪTH OF AL-BUKHĀRĪ AND MUSLIM
ON THE AUTHORITY OF ABŪ HURAYRAH.

189

O God, I seek Your protection from
misery and grief,
from weakness and laziness,
and from the burden of loans and from things
that will make others overcome me.

ḤADĪTH OF AL-BUKHĀRĪ AND MUSLIM
ON THE AUTHORITY OF ANAS IBN MĀLIK.

190

'Ā'ishah related how she heard the
Prophet praying thus:
'O God, be lenient with me while judging
me.'
When she asked him what leniency of
judgement meant, he said,
'God's forgiveness after He has seen a man's
record. O 'Ā'ishah, anyone who is judged
strictly will be ruined.'

ḤADĪTH OF AḤMAD IBN ḤANBAL.

191

According to Abū Saʿīd al-Khudrī,
the Prophet said,
'Whenever one of the faithful invokes
blessings which involve no sin or
the breaking up of a relationship,
God is certain to grant one of three things.
Either He gives the supplicant
His blessings in this world,
or He keeps them for him
in the world hereafter,
or He saves him from some misfortune.'
His listener then said,
'Now we shall invoke
God's blessings even more.'
'God's blessings are boundless,'
replied the Prophet.

ḤADĪTH OF AḤMAD IBN ḤANBAL.

192

This is the invocation of a troubled man:
'O Allah I am a petitioner for Divine Mercy.
Do not abandon me
even for a moment to any desires.
And keep all my affairs in order.
There is no God but
You.'

ḤADĪTH OF ABŪ DĀWŪD
ON THE AUTHORITY OF ABŪ BAKR.

193

God is nearest to His servant in the
last phase of the night.
If possible,
be one of those who remember
God during this period.

ḤADĪTH OF AT-TIRMIDHĪ
ON THE AUTHORITY OF 'AMR IBN 'ABASAH.

194

God extends His hand at night so that
He may accept the repentance of those
who indulge in wickedness during the day.
God extends His hand during the day so that
He may accept the repentance of those
who indulge in wickedness at night.
This will continue
till the sun rises in the west.

HADĪTH OF MUSLIM
ON THE AUTHORITY OF ABŪ MŪSĀ AL-ASH'ARĪ.

195

Those who remember God and
those who do not
are as different from each
other as the living and the dead.

HADĪTH OF AL-BUKHĀRĪ AND MUSLIM
ON THE AUTHORITY OF ABŪ MŪSĀ AL-ASH'ARĪ.

196

According to Tamīm ad‚Dārī,
the Prophet said,
'Well-wishing is faith.
Well-wishing is faith.
Well-wishing is faith.'
When asked towards whom,
he replied,
'Towards God,
His Messenger,
His Book,
the Muslim rulers
and
the common people.'

ḤADĪTH OF MUSLIM

197

Whenever the meal was concluded
the Prophet Muḥammad would say,
'Praise be to Allah,
in plenty,
in the best form
and in abundance.
The praise,
which we ourselves offer
and the praise
which does not desert us,
and whose desire never leaves us
and we do not become
indifferent to
praise (of God),
O Our Lord.'

ḤADĪTH OF AL-BUKHĀRĪ
ON THE AUTHORITY OF ABŪ UMĀMAH

198

God is bountiful and feels unhappy if He has to refuse to grant a wish. He feels embarrassed when a man holds out both his hands before Him, and He has to disappoint him by turning him away empty-handed.

HADĪTH OF ABŪ DĀWŪD AND AT-TIRMIDHĪ
ON THE AUTHORITY OF SALMĀN AL-FARSĪ.

199

'Abdullāh ibn Mas'ūd said, 'It is as if I see the Prophet Muḥammad ﷺ describing the life of one of the prophets,[1] who is assaulted by his people until the blood runs. He wipes the blood from his face and says, "O God, forgive my people for they know not what they do."'

HADĪTH OF BUKHĀRĪ AND MUSLIM.

1. THE ALLUSION IS PROBABLY MADE TO THE PROPHET NŪḤ (NOAH)(A.S.)

200

O God,
I seek divine guidance so that
I may remain steadfast in what is just.
I seek divine guidance in order
to be firm in righteousness.
I seek divine guidance in the manner
that I express my gratitude
for Your favours
and worship with devotion.
I seek from You a tongue
that speaks the truth
and a heart which is
pure and clean.

HADĪTH OF AT-TIRMIDHĪ.